Life As a
Chicken

Victoria Parker

Raintree

Chicago, Illinois

For information, address the publisher:
Raintree, 100 N. LaSalle, Suite 1200, Chicago, IL 60602

Printed and bound in the United States at Lake Book Manufacturing, Inc.
07 06 05 04 03
10 9 8 7 6 5 4 3 2 1

Library of Congress Cataloging-in-Publication Data:
Parker, Victoria.
   Life as a chicken / Victoria Parker.
      p. cm. -- (Life as)
Summary: Takes a comprehensive look at the characteristics of the
chicken, from egg to adult.
Includes bibliographical references and index.
   ISBN 1-4109-0630-2 (Library Binding-hardcover) -- ISBN 1-4109-0656-6 (Paperback)
   1. Chickens--Juvenile literature. [1. Chickens.] I. Title. II.
Series: Parker, Victoria.   Life as.
   SF487.5.P37 2004
   636.5--dc21

                                2003008120

Acknowledgments
The publishers would like to thank the following for permission to reproduce photographs: p. 16 Ardea; pp. 22, 23 Ardea (John Daniels); pp. 4, 11 Bruce Coleman (Jane Burton); pp. 14, 15 (Robert Maier); p. 6 Corbis; p. 13 FLPA (Roger Wilmshurst); p. 18 Nature Picture Library (William Osborn); p. 19 NHPA ; p. 10 NHPA (G I Bernard); pp. 20, 21 Oxford Scientific Films; pp. 8 OSF (Martyn Chillmaid); p. 12 (Tony Allen); p. 17 Woodfall Wild Images (E A Janes)

Cover photograph reproduced with permission of elektraVision/Index Stock Imagery

Every effort has been made to contact copyright holders of any material reproduced in this book. Any omissions will be rectified in subsequent printings if notice is given to the publishers.

Some words are shown in bold, **like this.** You can find out
what they mean by looking in the glossary on page 24.

Contents

A Nest of Eggs

Here are some eggs in a **nest**.

Where did these eggs come from?

Hens

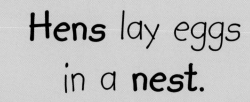

Hens lay eggs
in a **nest**.

They sit on the
eggs to keep
them warm.

Hatching

After a few weeks,
the eggs start to crack.

Chicks

Chicks come out of the eggs.
They are all wet.

The chicks dry off. They are covered with soft **down.**

11

A Chick's Life

Soon, the chicks can run around.

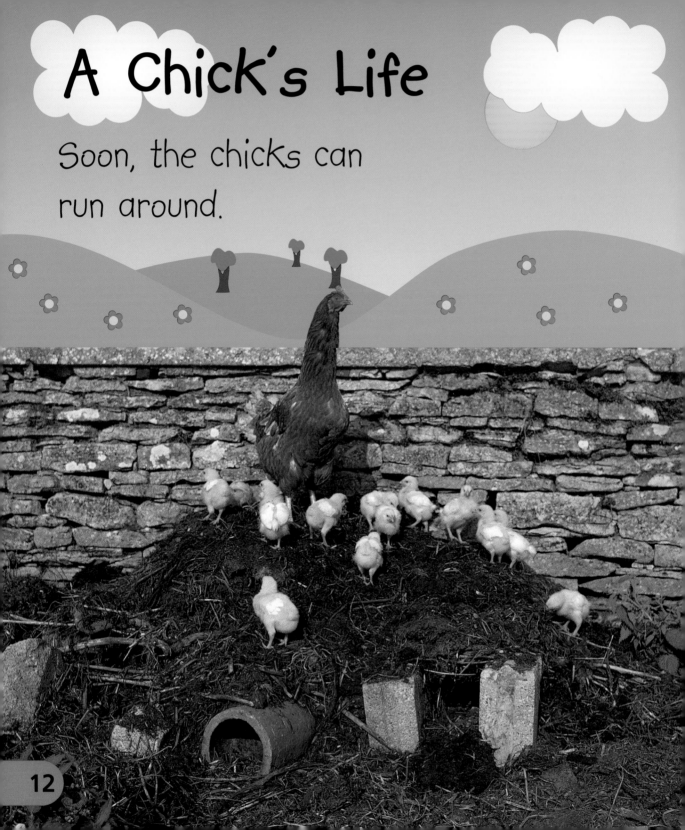

feed

The chicks stay near the **hen.**

They eat **feed.**

Growing

The chicks grow bigger.

14

From Chick
to Chicken

The chicks grow into chickens.
There are **roosters** and **hens.**

Roosters have **combs** on their heads.

Hens are smaller than roosters.

comb

rooster

hen

Day and Night

In the daytime, chickens look for food.

They scratch the dirt with their feet.

At night, chickens go to sleep.

They sleep in a **hen** house.

Laying Eggs

Some **hens** do not live with **roosters**.

There are no chicks inside the eggs they lay.

Other hens do live with roosters.
Their eggs have chicks inside.

New Chick Quiz

Where did these new chicks come from?

Look for the answers on page 24.

Glossary

comb   red skin on the top of a rooster's head

down   soft, yellow feathers that cover a new chick

feed   special food for chickens made from plants, such as corn or wheat

hatch   to come out of an egg

hen   girl chicken

nest   pile of twigs or straw that chickens and other birds make for their eggs

rooster   boy chicken

Chicken Life Cycle

Hens and **roosters** live together.

Hens lay eggs.

Chicks **hatch** from the eggs.

The chicks grow into hens and roosters.

This is where the new chicks on page 23 came from.

Index

24